Things That Go

Clive Gifford

KINGFISHER

NEW YORK

Distributed in the U.S. by Macmillan,
175 Fifth Ave., New York, NY 10010

Library of Congress Cataloging-in-Publication data
has been applied for.

Illustrations by Peter Bull Art Studio

ISBN: 978-0-7534-6593-6

Kingfisher books are available for special promotions
and premiums. For details contact: Special Markets
Department, Macmillan, 175 Fifth Ave.,
New York, NY 10010.

For more information, please visit
www.kingfisherbooks.com

Printed in China
1 3 5 7 9 8 6 4 2
1TR/0211/WKT/UNTD/115MA

Picture credits

**The Publisher would like to thank the following
for permission to reproduce their images
(t = top, b = bottom, c = center, r = right, l = left):**

Page 4tr Shutterstock/Marcel Jancovic; 4cl Corbis/Patrick
Chauvel; 4b Shutterstock/Greenland; 5tr Shutterstock/Karen
Hadley; 5cl Shutterstock/LWPhotography; 5bl Shutterstock/Maksim
Toome; 5br Shutterstock/Teodor Ostojlc; 10bl Shutterstock/Stuart
Monk; 12–13 Photolibrary/Japan Travel Bureau; 12bl Shutterstock/
Christine F.; 12c Shutterstock/Peter Gudelia; 12br Getty/AFP;
13tr Shutterstock/Binkski; 13br Getty/Anatole Antoniol; 16b
Photolibrary/White; 17tr Shutterstock/Javier Sanchez; 17ctl Alamy/
Frans Lemmons; 17cb Alamy/Colin Underhill; 18tl Shutterstock/
alterfalter; 20c Shutterstock/Denis Klimov; 20bl Corbis/Brooks
Kraft; 21tl Corbis/Randy Jolly; 21tr Shutterstock/Xin Qiu; 21cr
Shutterstock/Patrick Wang; 21br Shutterstock/oblong1; 22bl
Shutterstock/Wally Sternberger; 24c Alamy/Kuttig-People;
24bl Alamy/Paul Carstairs; 24br Shutterstock/iPhotos;
25tl Corbis/Guido Cozzi; 25tr Corbis/jkm AP; 25b Corbis/Jeffrey
Rotman; 26bl Science Photo Library/STARSEM; 28c Reuters/STR
New; 28cr Corbis/Reuters/China Daily; 28bl Corbis/Marc Sanchez;
29t Getty/George Hall/Check Six; 29bl XSGM World Ltd.;
29r ESA/NASA; 30tr Alamy/rshantz; 30ctl Shutterstock/Scott
Scheibelhut; 30ctr Shutterstock/Neo Edmund; 30cbr Alamy/David
Hancock; 30bl Reuters/Petr Josek Snr.; 30br Shutterstock/eddtoro;
31tl Shutterstock/T. H. Klimmeck; 31tr Alamy/Friederich Saurer;
31ctr Shutterstock/SVLuma; 31cbl Shutterstock/Pavel Losevsky;
31br Alamy/Cultura

Contents

More to explore

On some of the pages in this book, you will find colored buttons with symbols on them. There are four different colors, and each belongs to a different topic. Choose a topic, follow its colored buttons through the book, and you'll make some interesting discoveries of your own.

For example, on page 6 you'll find an orange button, like this, next to a picture of a racecar. The orange buttons are about engine power.

Page 15

Engine power

There is a page number in the button. Turn to that page (page 15) to find an orange button next to something else about engine power. Follow all the steps through the book, and at the end of your journey you'll find out how the steps are linked and discover even more information about this topic.

Science

Safety first

People

The other topics in this book are science, safety first, and people. Follow the steps and see what you can discover!

Machines on the move

Machines that help us move from place to place are known as vehicles. Large vehicles, such as trains and ships, can move many people or goods at once. Smaller vehicles, such as motorcycles, may carry only one person at a time.

A cycle rickshaw carries schoolchildren through a city.

People ride in a cart attached to the bike.

Carts, sleds, and wagons can be moved by animals. People around the world still use horses, donkeys, oxen, and dogs to pull these vehicles across the ground.

Some vehicles are **powered by people**. On a bicycle, the rider pushes the pedals around with his or her feet and legs. The pedals turn a chain, which turns the back wheel around. This moves the bicycle forward.

A bicyclist turns the handlebars to steer the bicycle.

The handlebars turn the front wheel left or right.

chain

pedal

Motor vehicles have engines, or motors, to give them power. The engine turns the back wheel of a motorcycle like the one below. Cars, buses, and trucks are motor vehicles, too.

an aircraft display team

A motorcycle racer speeds along a dirt track.

Aircraft fly through the air. Some are huge airliners that can carry hundreds of people across the world in a single flight. Other aircraft hold only one or two people.

Sports cars have powerful engines to help them travel fast.

Wind catches in a yacht's sails.

The engine is underneath the hood.

Boats and ships float on rivers, lakes, and oceans. Some are powered by an engine or by people pulling oars through the water. Others use the power of the wind to push them along.

What is this?

1 crash barrier

2 Mechanics change a tire in the pit.

3 A checkered flag signals the winner.

Page 27

Page 15

Daring racers

Ever since cars were invented, people have loved racing them. Today's Formula One racecars are super fast. They can reach up to 250 mph (400km/h)—that's about four times the speed allowed on highways! Thousands of fans gather to watch them race.

2

3

Page 18

5

4

6

After 90 minutes of tough racing, car number 4 zooms across the finish line. It has won the race by less than a second! A Formula One race lasts 60–70 laps of the twisting, turning track. If a car has a problem, the driver can steer it off the track and into the pit. There, the driver's team will fix the car or change the tires—but they need to be quick!

This is the steering wheel of a Formula One car.

How cars go

A car is powered by an engine. The engine
turns the car's wheels, moving the car forward.
A driver can speed up the car by pressing
a foot pedal called the accelerator.
Pressing the brake pedal slows
the car down or stops it.

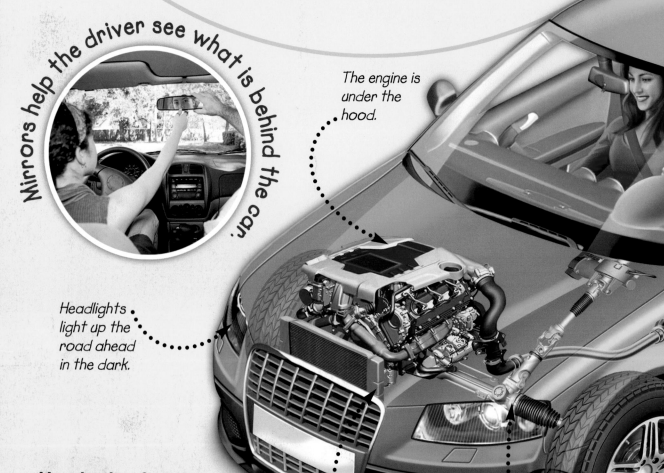

Mirrors help the driver see what is behind the car.

The engine is
under the
hood.

Headlights
light up the
road ahead
in the dark.

Hundreds of parts
make up a modern
automobile. The frame of the
car is called the chassis. Other
big parts, such as the engine,
doors, and body panels, are
attached to the chassis.

The radiator cools
down the engine.

The steering wheel
connects to the axle
to turn the wheels.

A driver refuels his car at a pump.

Seat belts keep people safely strapped in their seats.

Most car engines work by burning **fuel** such as gasoline or diesel. This releases some harmful gases into the air. Some new cars have electric motors that run on battery power instead.

An electric car recharges its batteries.

Gases from the engine come out of the exhaust pipe.

Bumpers protect the front and back of a car.

Tires help the wheels grip the road.

To start a car, the driver turns the ignition key. This fires small sparks inside the engine and gets the car running. At the end of a trip, the driver turns the key again to stop the engine.

Cars travel on road networks that link many different places.

Roads are busy places, and drivers need to know how to use them safely. Signs warn drivers not to drive more than a certain speed. Signals such as traffic lights tell vehicles to stop to let other cars or people cross a street.

Transportation in town

Every day, millions of people make trips across towns and cities. Some people walk or ride bicycles, while others drive cars. Public transportation vehicles, such as buses, streetcars, and trains, move many people at once. Traffic signals help keep streets and railroads safe.

Page 30

What is this?

1. A bus stops to let people on or off.
2. A streetcar travels along a track.
3. monorail train

? A traffic light shines green. This tells vehicles that they can move ahead.

In this busy city, roads are not the only places for machines on the move. Above the streets, a monorail train cruises along a high track. Below the streets, subway trains carry people through underground tunnels. Both subway and monorail trains stop at station platforms where passengers can get on and off.

3

4

5

Page 27

6

4 traffic policeman on a motorcycle

5 escalator to and from the subway

6 Subway trains arrive at a platform.

On track

Trains run on railroad tracks from one place to another. Their wheels have a special shape that fits over the rails and keeps them on the tracks. At the front of a train is a locomotive engine. This can pull many railroad cars behind it.

Steam trains get their power from steam, which is made by heating water in a big boiler. The steam pushes parts of the steam engine, making it turn the wheels around.

Tracks are made of long rails and shorter ties.

rail   tie

This high-speed train is called a bullet train.

These people are inside a city subway train.

Steam puffs out of the train's chimney.

This freight train uses diesel to power its engine.

Bullet trains are powered by electric cables.

Up to 1,300 passengers can travel in the train's cars.

Trains don't only carry people; they pull heavy loads, too. **Freight trains** move materials such as sand or coal across the country. Some freight trains are very long and can be made up of 50 or more cars.

The driver controls the train from the cab.

The fastest trains that carry passengers are called bullet trains. They were first built in Japan and can travel at more than 170 mph (275km/h).

Underground trains travel through long tunnels below the ground, mostly in busy cities. Some trains go through tunnels under the water. Eurotunnel trains carry people, and even cars, under the ocean between England and France.

① concrete mixer

② A crane lifts heavy steel girders.

③ The girders arrived here on a truck.

What is this?

Heavyweight vehicles

People use huge vehicles to build things such as houses, offices, bridges, and roads. Trucks carry materials to a construction site. Forklifts, cranes, and front-end loaders move these materials around. Cranes lift loads up high, and excavators reach low to dig big holes in the ground.

4 forklift

5 An excavator
   digs holes.

6 dump truck

7 A front-end loader
   scoops up dirt.

15

5

6

1

Page 18

Page 23

At this noisy construction site, trucks deliver girders and bricks while other vehicles move them around. A dump truck tips sand out of its trailer. Some of this will be taken to the concrete mixer, where it will be churned with other materials to make concrete.

This is a close-up of the tread on a truck's tire, which helps it grip the ground.

Carrying heavy loads

Some vehicles are built to carry very large or heavy things. These machines have to be super tough. They need big, powerful engines so that they can transport their loads—which may be heavy firefighting equipment or even a house!

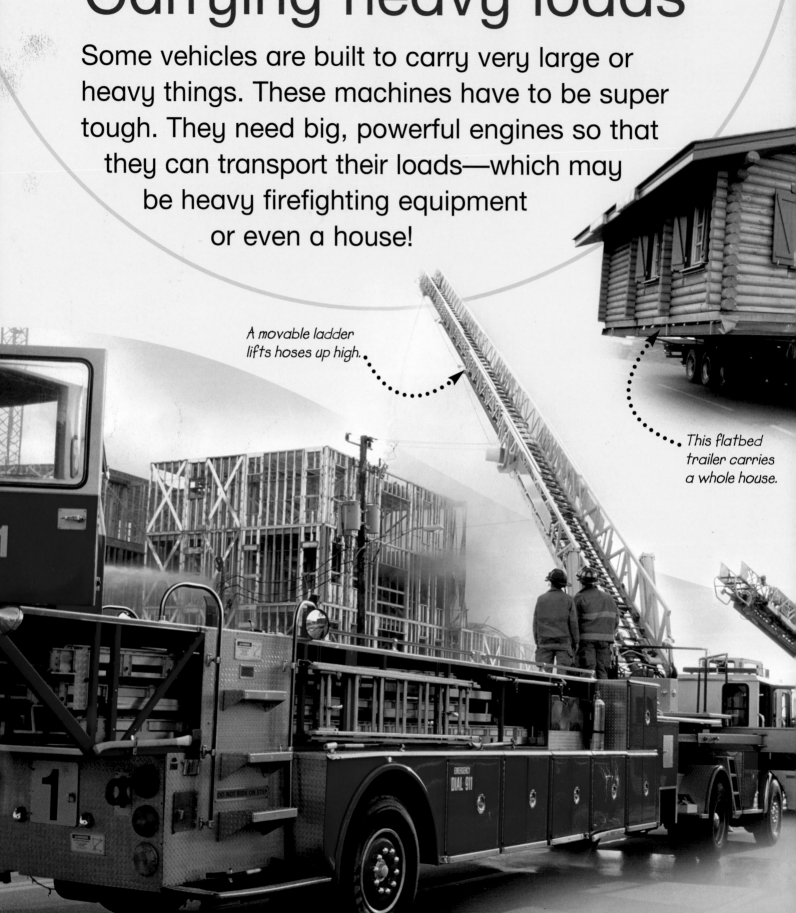

A movable ladder lifts hoses up high.

This flatbed trailer carries a whole house.

Semitrailer trucks have a driver's cab that can be attached to different trailers. Some trailers are box shaped and can hold goods inside. Flatbed trailers are flat with no sides, so large loads can rest on top.

A road train travels through Australia.

Road trains have a powerful cab that can pull two, three, or more trailers at once. They are used to transport things long distances through areas with few towns.

Giant dump trucks are used in mining to move large loads of rock.

The engine is in the cab part, giving it power to pull the trailer.

The driver looks tiny next to these 10-ft. (3-m) wheels!

Fire engines carry water, ladders, pumps, and other firefighting equipment quickly to a fire. Their ladders stretch upward to reach fires or to rescue people trapped in tall buildings.

Car transporters move cars from the factories where they were made to show rooms where they go on sale. This transporter carries ten cars, all fixed securely in place.

What is this?

1 A marshaller directs a plane.

2 wheels for takeoff and landing

3 pilot in the cockpit

4 truck with trailer full of luggage

Page 22

Page 26

High fliers

Aircraft fly all over the world, taking off and landing on flat, smooth strips called runways. Airports often have more than one runway so that several planes can take off and land at the same time. On the ground, other vehicles help transport passengers and their luggage around.

Page 30

An aircraft speeds along the runway, takes off, and flies into the air. Inside the cockpit, the pilot is in control. He must fly safely over land and water to another airport where the plane will land. Passengers from a larger aircraft are disembarking in the background. They've arrived for their vacation! A staircase has been wheeled over to let them off the plane.

This is a propeller. It spins around very fast and helps power an airplane through the sky.

Takeoff

An aircraft starts its journey by moving faster and faster across the ground. Air flows over the aircraft's wings, which helps lift it off the runway and up into the air. Giant jet engines give the plane power to speed along.

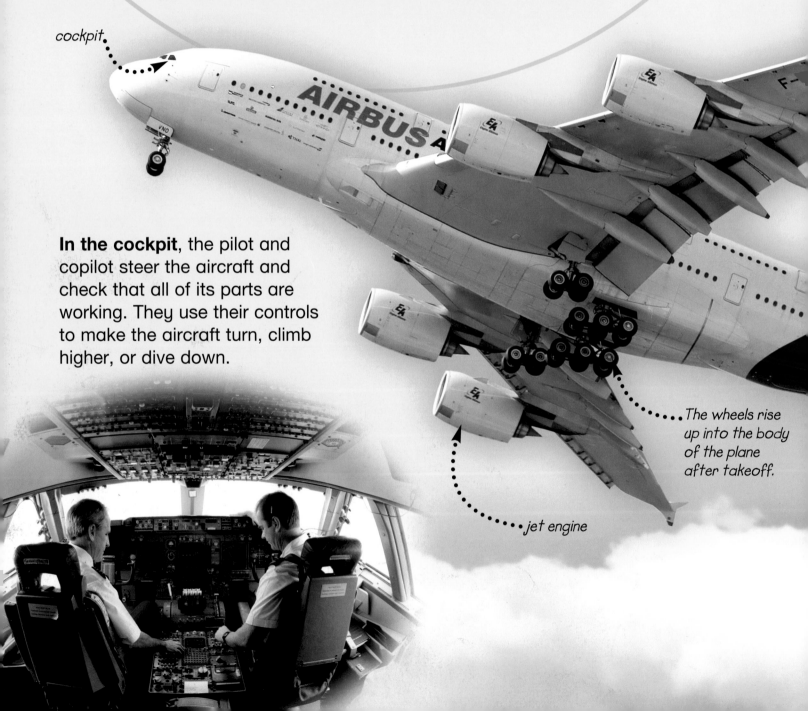

cockpit

In the cockpit, the pilot and copilot steer the aircraft and check that all of its parts are working. They use their controls to make the aircraft turn, climb higher, or dive down.

The wheels rise up into the body of the plane after takeoff.

jet engine

Jet engines thrust out hot gases, forcing the plane forward.

Hot-air balloons are filled with air that is heated by a burner. The warm air rises, carrying the balloons up into the sky.

Passengers ride in the basket.

A helicopter hovers to rescue a person in trouble.

A large airliner like this one needs a lot of power to speed along the runway and rise up into the air. This power comes from four huge jet engines, located underneath the wings.

A38

Elevator flaps help the plane fly up or down.

The body of a plane is called the fuselage.

Rotor blades spin to let the helicopter hover in midair.

Seaplanes can take off from lakes, rivers, and oceans. Instead of wheels, they have large floats full of air. These allow the planes to rest on the surface of the water.

Riding the waves

Ships and boats travel the waters of the world. They take people on fun trips and carry passengers and their cars across rivers and oceans. Many ships move large amounts of goods, called cargo. They sail into ports or harbors, where they can transfer their loads to or from land.

2574

① Page 10

What is this?

① catamaran, a type of sailboat

② fishing trawler

③ A tugboat tows larger boats in and out of the harbor.

? This is a boat anchor. It is dropped to the bottom of the water to keep the boat still.

6

5

75632

Page 19

Page 30

This harbor is full of action, with boats cruising in and out from the ocean. A family has fun on a speedboat while other people are hard at work. Fishermen on a trawler pull in their nets. A huge container ship unloads its cargo. The colored crates contain goods that will go on to travel by truck or train.

ISABELLA

4 A speedboat prepares to race away.

5 A coast-guard boat checks that everyone is safe on the water.

6 Cranes unload a giant container ship.

Floating and diving

Boats and ships float on top of the water. Their shapes push away the water and keep them above the surface. Boats come in many shapes and sizes, but they must be carefully made so that they don't tip over or sink.

This rubber boat is filled with air.

Boats float because they are lighter than the water they push away. Some materials, such as wood, float naturally. Other materials can be made to float by filling them with air. Air is much lighter than water, so boats can carry people and still not sink.

Paddling pushes the water back, which moves the boat forward.

Amphibious vehicles can travel on both land and water.

wheels for use on land

The body of a boat is called its **hull**. The boat's hull presses down on the water and the water pushes back. This keeps the boat afloat.

hull

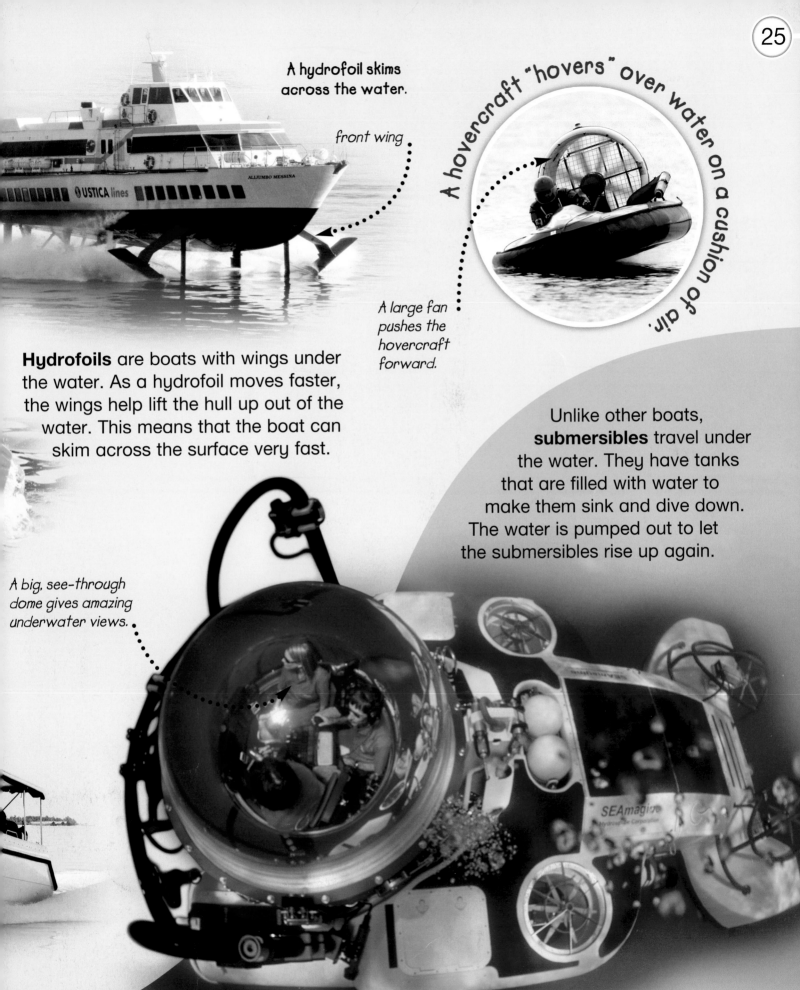

A hydrofoil skims across the water.

front wing

A hovercraft "hovers" over water on a cushion of air.

A large fan pushes the hovercraft forward.

Hydrofoils are boats with wings under the water. As a hydrofoil moves faster, the wings help lift the hull up out of the water. This means that the boat can skim across the surface very fast.

Unlike other boats, **submersibles** travel under the water. They have tanks that are filled with water to make them sink and dive down. The water is pumped out to let the submersibles rise up again.

A big, see-through dome gives amazing underwater views.

SEAmagine

Really fast rockets

A space rocket blasts hot gases downward to thrust itself up into the sky. The blast is enough to drive the rocket away from Earth and far off into space. Inside the rocket is its payload. This may be a satellite that takes pictures of Earth, or it may even be astronauts on a space mission.

Page 30

What is this?

1 This transporter carried the rocket to its launch pad.

2 The launch pad is hidden by gases from the exhausts.

3 The main rocket is over 130 ft. (40m) tall.

? These are exhaust tubes at the bottom of a rocket, where the hot gases blast out.

6

Page 23

5

Page 15

Five . . . four . . . three . . . two . . . one . . . LIFTOFF! A giant space rocket shoots into the air as its engines fire. Clouds of hot gases blast out of the exhaust tubes, lifting the rocket upward. At first, the rocket rises slowly because of its great weight. It will soon start to build up speed so that it zooms into space very fast.

4 Booster rockets give launch power but fall away soon after liftoff.

5 This rocket carries a satellite as its payload.

6 space-center buildings

Record breakers

Some people try to build machines that go faster than ever before. These record-breaking vehicles need very powerful engines. They need a smooth, sleek body to zoom through the air, water, or space. They also need a brave driver!

ThrustSSC is the world's fastest machine on land. In 1997, it raced across a flat desert and reached an amazing speed of 763 mph (1,228km/h). It was powered by two jet engines, normally used in jet fighter planes.

The fastest racecars are called Top Fuel dragsters. These cars race in pairs along a straight piece of track. They finish their 1,300-ft. (400-m)-long race in less than five seconds. Wow!

A TGV train in France once traveled at more than 350 mph (570km/h).

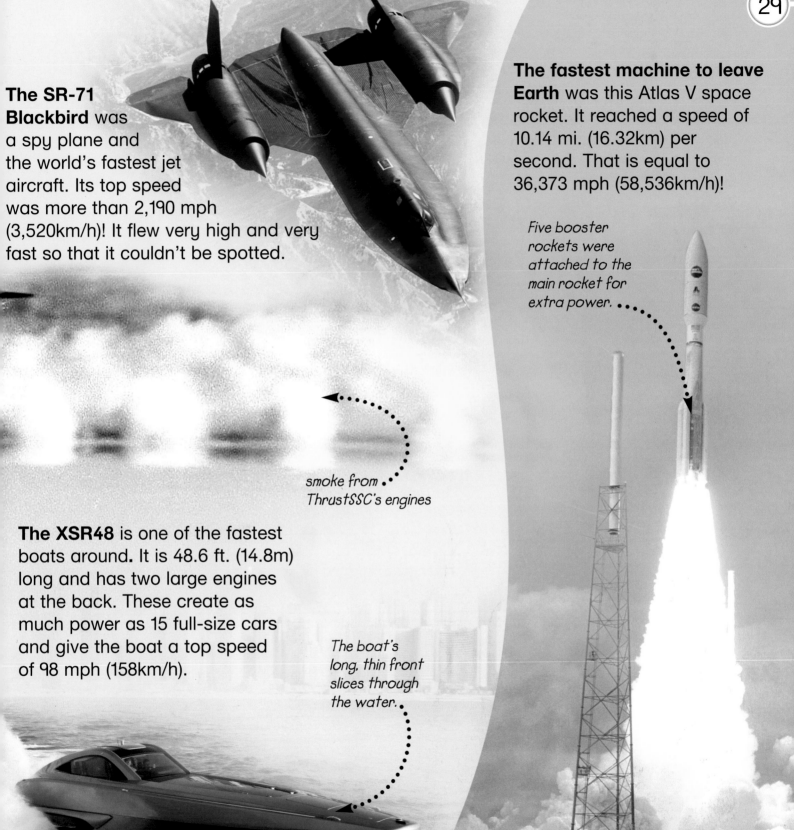

The SR-71 Blackbird was a spy plane and the world's fastest jet aircraft. Its top speed was more than 2,190 mph (3,520km/h)! It flew very high and very fast so that it couldn't be spotted.

The fastest machine to leave Earth was this Atlas V space rocket. It reached a speed of 10.14 mi. (16.32km) per second. That is equal to 36,373 mph (58,536km/h)!

Five booster rockets were attached to the main rocket for extra power.

smoke from ThrustSSC's engines

The XSR48 is one of the fastest boats around. It is 48.6 ft. (14.8m) long and has two large engines at the back. These create as much power as 15 full-size cars and give the boat a top speed of 98 mph (158km/h).

The boat's long, thin front slices through the water.

XSR48 superboat

Engine power

A Formula One car engine is very powerful. It enables the car to **accelerate** (speed up) from sitting still to 125 mph (200km/h) in less than four seconds!

The world's **largest dump trucks** are more than 50 ft. (15m) long and 23 ft. (7m) tall. Their giant engines give them power to carry up to 400 tons of rock—that is heavier than 50 adult elephants!

Science

Racecars have a smooth shape so that air flows easily around their bodies. This is called **streamlining**. It helps the vehicles race forward more quickly.

Rockets send space **satellites** high up above Earth's surface. There, they travel in a big circle around the planet. Some satellites are used to bounce TV pictures or telephone calls from one part of the world to another.

Safety first

A **strong harness** straps a racecar driver firmly into the seat. The driver wears a special suit that protects against flames if there is a fire. A helmet protects the head.

Before a plane takes off, staff onboard carry out a **safety demonstration**. They show passengers how to fasten their seat belts and what to do if there is a problem during the flight.

People

The driver of a bus, train, or streetcar follows a set route and schedule to get passengers to the right place at the right time. He or she stays in touch with station workers by radio, reporting any problems along the way.

Astronauts are people who travel into space. Mission controllers stay on Earth but follow a space rocket's journey. They check that all goes well and can sometimes send radio signals to the rocket to change its course.

More to explore

Huge passenger airliners have four or more powerful jet engines. The biggest of all is the **Airbus A380**, which can carry up to 850 people. Its top speed is just over 620 mph (1,000km/h)!

The engines of the **Saturn V space rocket** packed more power than 300,000 sports cars! Saturn V was as tall as a 36-story building. From liftoff, it took only two and a half minutes to climb 42 mi. (68km) into the sky.

Caterpillar tracks are added to many heavy vehicles to stop them from sinking into soft or muddy ground. The tracks work by spreading the weight of a vehicle over a larger area than an ordinary wheel and tire.

A **rudder** is a flat fin that is attached to the back of a boat. It sits under the water and is used for steering. Pushing the rudder one way or the other changes the flow of water around the boat and helps it turn.

Many people on boats wear **life jackets**. These are full of either air or a very light material such as foam, which floats well in water. Life jackets help stop people from sinking under the water if they fall in.

Bicycle lanes are parts of roads that are marked especially for bicycles. They separate the bicyclists from the other traffic and help keep them safe. Bicycle lanes are found in many big towns and cities.

Coast guards try to keep everyone safe at sea. Sometimes, they rush out of the harbor to help a boat or swimmer in trouble. At other times, they check on boat safety or help fight crimes on the water.

Air-traffic controllers plot the direction and height above the ground at which aircraft are flying. They talk to pilots on the radio and help guide them in to land safely.

Index